Our Lives with Dogs

By Janice Hoffmann
and Laurence Hoffmann

PREFACE

I think the dogs I've known and loved, the dogs I've lived with, have a lot in common with the dogs you've known and loved, the dogs you've lived with, or fantasized about living with. This book is dedicated to them.

Massimo, my sixth dog, the fourth Maltese Larry and I have raised together, was born on January 6, 2022. By the time Our Lives with Dogs is published, he will be about two in dog years, a teenager in people's parlance. You will meet him at the end of this book in the chapter entitled "Massimo Speaks."

Our third Maltese, **Carina**, was named so that when she met our Italian daughters, they would say how cute she was in Italian, thus intuiting her name. "Ah! Carina!" they would exclaim upon seeing her. Carina enjoyed our affection for over a dozen years and is the heroine of this book, appearing in all of the stories and limerick collections until Massimo is introduced in the penultimate section. She is a stand-in for all the dogs that have understood you better than your human friends.

Our first two were named Theodore Roosevelt, because Teddy was an adventurous teddy bear, and Eleanor Roosevelt, because Miss Ellie was a formidable female who accomplished lots, doing what she wanted, when she wanted. Teddy and Miss Ellie came to live with us after our sons, Eric and Gabe, went into the world to seek their fortunes, and our nest was quite empty and our household quite quiet.

Before I met Larry 40 years ago, there had been two dogs in my life: 1) Aphrodite, a wise black lab who kept me safe as she and I camped in a pup tent on the East Coast, driving from Vermont to South Carolina to interview for grad school, and 2) Laddie, a collie/Australian shepherd who was my companion from my age six months to when I drove me first car. Laddie was my first teacher about love and loss.

I met dog photographer Diana Lundin in 2015, when she photographed Carina at home, at the beach, and at the California Botanic Garden when you could buy a limited doggy pass as a fundraiser. You'll see her photographs throughout the book, including the cover.

I wrote the prose, and my husband Larry is the chief limericist, my trusted editor and advisor.

If you like dogs and always need a fix of feel-good dog stories and photos to put a smile on your face, this book is for you.

print ISBN: 979-8-35097-368-6

ebook ISBN: 979-8-35097-369-3

Contents

MY FIRST DAY
WITHOUT CARINA

Lama Rod Owens reminds us that when we grieve for someone, we feel the pain of a loss of our own identity, who we were when our life was inextricably intertwined with whomever or whatever we lost. For 14 years, I had identified as Carina's mom. I'd been that person with the cute little dog, the five-pound wonder photographed on a skateboard, on a fishing boat wearing a life vest, caught mid-stride, all four legs aloft while flying-running on the beach, wearing her own participant number at the Rotary 5kTurkey Trot, posing with great dignity atop a Steinway, pausing patiently as a little girl experiences a momentary lapful of dog, lounging in wheelchair laps at Pilgrim Place Health Services Center, carefully sounding out a note with a front paw on the piano.

She was the dog made famous in over 50 limericks my husband wrote,

There once was a dog named Carina,
who had a most pleasant demeanor.
She was tiny and cute,
with a soft tail to boot.
You'd like her if ever you'd seen her.

Carina was so very dear.
She brought us joy year after year.
But then she got sick,
and the end came quite quick,
but for us, she will always be near

Once Carina left us, we no longer had an automatic conversation starter to describe ourselves, and there was no built-in buffer. Carina had been a good listener, so now there were fewer idle conversations and fewer opportunities to delve deep into issues:

"Carina, are you ready to go outside? Ask Daddy if he would take you out before dinner."

"Don't look at me like that, I don't understand cryptocurrency either."

"How do you like your new playlist? The 174 Hz Sound Bath is for pain".

Wish we knew what went on in her brain.
Just think of the knowledge we'd gain.
Was she thinking of walks,
or perhaps some TED talks?
That's assuming, of course, she was sane.

But near the end, it was a lot: daily prescriptions, .25 ml of this, .5 ml of that; mixing probiotics and omega-3s into her homemade dog food; breaking up freeze-dried minnows into even tinier pieces and burying them under dog food, one of the few games that still brought her joy. For some reason, in the weeks preceding her death, she would only chow down if her food was taken out of her bowl and spread around her placemat, so that became our mealtime ritual, anything to keep her eating. Every day, we tried to help her find what might bring her peace in the late afternoon when she couldn't get comfortable, and everyone got the blues. The vet had given up. We needed to let go. It was a lot. For her. For me. For us.

Janice Hoffmann & Laurence Hoffmann

A few days before Angel Veterinary Services was scheduled to come to our home to help us let her go, I took her on one last walk, her favorite route through the playground in Higgenbotham Park, but this time she led me where we had never gone before. Together we walked through a culvert. It was very uncomfortable for me to duck that low, but she led me to the other side, and a few days later she crossed to the other side without me. The hole that remains is plugged with poignant memories.

"...though I dream in vain, in my heart it will remain
my Stardust melody, a memory of love's refrain."

-Hoagy Carmichael/Mitchell Parish

AN OPEN LETTER TO OUR CALIFORNIA BLACK BEARS

To the Mamas and the Papas,

The Claraboya Homeowners Association has asked me to bring to your attention long-established protocols that we've been following. Due to the unique circumstances of the recent pandemic, Claraboya residents spent over a year without hiking the Wilderness Park trail. Just like our human youngsters, the lack of human contact experienced by your youngsters has negative consequences. Not having been steeped in the traditions of coexistence, your cubs have been exhibiting some frightening *rumsp ringa* behaviors.

Our HOA CC&Rs expressly prohibit bears from emerging from your lairs before dark. Last night, my Carina and I were one house-length away from turning into the Via Sinaloa cul-de-sac when two of your cubs came bounding out. They were gamboling across Via Espirito Santos with reckless abandon and had no regard for humans or canines. It was not even dusk, let alone dark, and we have the right to the streets until nightfall. (See HOA CC&Rs, Section VI. paragraph 3.)

If allowed to continue, this behavior can be harmful. We simply won't stand for it. A week from Thursday at 7 p.m., the HOA will convene a special meeting at the Hughes Community Center to condemn this behavior. If you have anything to say, you can show up then.

In the meantime, while I have your attention, before you embark on your Tuesday night romp preceding Wednesday morning trash pickup, bear in mind that each paw is unique and bears the identity of anyone who attempts to remain anonymous. I know who you are. Your muddy pawprints remain a stain on my stucco wall, so please stop it or use the disposable paw condoms I left for your convenience.

Furthermore, for your information, I never throw away berries or anything else fairy tales say you enjoy eating. I am a reformed vegan, and I remain stolidly plant-forward. However, the owners of a McDonalds live on our street, and I have numerous carnivorous neighbors. If you insist on dumpster diving, their garbage will likely be tastier than mine.

Oh, and before I go, I can't help it. I feel as if I must pay you a compliment. It's pretty amazing how you can balance your broad 300-pound behind atop my thin wrought iron fence while you feast from my bird feeders; however, you had better hope that somebody from Ringling Brothers wasn't scouting the neighborhood.

Sincerely,
Golden Lockes-Hoffmann
Special Contributor to the Claraboya HOA

P.S. In one photo, you look like you'd like to come and join us on the back patio. We'll talk. Maybe we can work something out.

CARINA AND MOMMY

"Come!"

Carina opens one eye.

Mommy repeats, "Come!" and assumes her best I-mean-business stance and stare. Both freeze as they watch each other, motionless. Who will cave first?

When Carina hears "Come!" she stops and thinks. When you weigh five pounds and vaguely resemble a powder puff, it's hard to be taken seriously, and today, it is particularly annoying, even if Mommy does want to go for our morning walk, because isn't it obvious that Carina is currently involved with Dolly?

Dolly, Carina's doppelgänger, was once a beautiful cream-colored stuffed kitty cat with head held high but now is a lifeless, dingy ragamuffin that Carina carries by the nape of the neck from room to room only to cuddle and lick upon arrival to the next of many dog beds. In their world, utter domination paired with utter devotion is a perfect symbiosis.

Carina ponders, grasping her Earth Animal No-Hide Venison Bone, soothing the absence of a back molar as she chews the mushy end. This calms her as she thinks, never breaking eye contact. What she does next will tip the balance of power.

She knows what the word "come" means. For god's sake, they have been playing this charade since puppy pre-school 12 years ago, and her patience is wearing thin. Do they have to do this to their dying day? Who cares who comes first? Isn't it more a matter of who goes first?

How much longer can she work this situation without Mommy engaging the GPS tracker which makes such a darn racket it hurts her ears and she has trouble holding her pee? Whenever The Tile goes off, she can't help herself. She runs straight to Mommy to turn it off. She is running out of time but continues to gnaw and doesn't flinch.

Mommy retreats and returns with a leash.

Carina sits and knows she is sitting.

Mommy stands and knows she is standing.

The luxury of time once again on her side, Carina rises and slowly performs her perfected down dog followed by the canine version of cat-cow, knowing that Mommy is a sucker for this routine.

Their standoff momentarily set aside, they begin their morning regimen, taking back Mountain Avenue with confidence and optimism, with only whiffs of bears and bobcats to remind them they can only walk in the daytime.

CARINA'S DOGGEREL

First appearing in England in the 1700s and popularized by Edward Lear in the 19th century, limericks are often rude to the point of bawdy. George Bernard Shaw described clean limericks as "rarely rising above mediocrity." however, "Carina's Doggerel," as told to her dad Larry, offers great wordplay with PG-13 humor; however, some must be read with a New York accent to rhyme. The subject mainly includes the challenges of an elderly dog aging with her elderly Mommy and Daddy.

There once was a dog named Carina,
who had a most pleasant demeanor.
She was tiny and cute,
with a soft tail to boot.
You'd like her if ever you'd seen her.

Carina's breed started in Malta,
not Corfu or Guam or Gibraltar,
but with other Maltese
she was quite hard to please,
and from barking, her mom had to halt her.

Carina was really quite pretty.
She ranked near the top in the city.
It made her so proud,
she would shout it out loud,
so she asked Dad to publish this ditty.

Carina was proud of her name,
but some people forgot. What a shame!
When they called her Serena,
or even Katrina,
she was kind and did not assign blame.

Carina the Maltese lived with her humans, Larry and Janice, for over a dozen years in the Claraboya neighborhood in the Southern California village of Claremont. Many of the limericks reflect life at home in their wildlife-rich Claraboya neighborhood.

There was a dog living in Claremont
in a house as big as the Fairmont,
but she saw a large bear
that gave her a scare,
so she started to call her home Bearmont

Carina knew she should not stare
if she ever met up with a bear.
She should make herself tall,
(which is hard if you're small)
and leave without any fanfare.

Carina knew what steps to take
if she ever ran into a snake.
She would stop in her track
and slowly walk back,
and try hard not to make a mistake.

Carina was happy to walk
when there was no owl or no hawk.
Before it got dark
she would stroll in the park
while Mommy and Daddy would talk.

Carina knew just how to act
if a coyote appeared in her track
It's gaze she would hold,
and appear large and bold,
then ask Mommy to carry her back.

The neighbor dog's bark was a pain
so Carina barked back to complain,
but the other barked more
and Carina would roar.
The situation was really insane.

This little white dog lived on Mountain
in a big house that featured a fountain.
There was art on the walls,
in the rooms and the halls,
just like in the Abbey of Downton.

Carina laid down like a Sphinx
not like a chinchilla or lynx.
She had a blank stare
as if she wasn't quite there,
or perhaps had too many drinks.

Carina did not like the doorbell.
With her, the sound never did score well.
She'd bark her head off
till she started to cough,
even at people she knew well.

Carina did not mind the groomer,
so she usually went with good humor.
They would brush and would wash
till she looked really posh,
but she told them not to perfume her.

The delivery truck dropped off a bag,
and Carina's tail started to wag.
There were minnows and bones,
and for mom, some iPhones.
This was really exceptional swag.

Wish we knew what went on in her brain.
Just think of the knowledge we'd gain.
Was she thinking of walks,
or perhaps some TED talks?
That's assuming, of course, that she's sane.

Carina the dog studied spelling
with her mommy and dad in their dwelling.
There were K-words like KAT,
and N-words like GNAT,
so many her head started swelling.

Carina was nobody's fool,
though she'd not attended a school.
She learned a few tricks,
chased after thrown sticks,
and tried to obey every rule.

Carina the dog loved her dolly.
What they did when together, "Oh, golly!"
They would bump and would hump,
and when done they would jump.
As a couple, they were always quite jolly.

There once was a dog who did yoga.
She didn't need shoes or a toga.
She did down dog and sit,
and rolled over a bit,
and found that the practice consoled her.

There once was a dog named Carina,
who thought other's grass might be greener.
Then she learned of the drought
and how green lawns were out,
so, about her brown yard was much keener.

Sniffing the ground was her hallmark,
so much she resembled an aardvark.
When she smelled something good,
as often she would,
she would let out an ear-piercing dog bark.

A little white dog wouldn't fetch.
When asked, she would grumble and kvetch.
When thrown a ball,
she would run down the hall,
but always preferred to play catch.

This little white dog goes to market.
She takes Mommy's car and she parks it.
She buys minnows and meat,
all she needs for a treat,
and to show she is thankful, she barks it.

There once was a dog named Carina,
who really like eating her dinner.
When told she'd get fat,
she said, "What's wrong with that?
I really don't need to be thinner.

There once was a person named mummy,
who took very good care of dog's tummy.
She would fill up the bowl
with rice casserole
and always made sure it was yummy.

Carina had a keen sense of smell,
with which there's so much she could tell,
like a plant or a tree
or another dog's pee.
Her nose served her really quite well.

Every year, Janice and Larry spend a week in dog-friendly Carmel, where they frequent Doris Day's Cypress Inn. The inn is noted for its after-dinner piano bar, which features great music, and most of the audience members bring their dogs. However, Carina's parents sometimes traveled without her, like when they went to Germany and Amsterdam for Christmas.

Carina's composure would crack
when Mommy and Daddy would pack.
It upset her tummy
and made her feel funny.
She feared they could never come back.

Carina's folks went off to Dortmund.
She wanted to go, but she couldn't.
It made her feel sad,
but it wasn't so bad,
since they weren't coming home with a dachshund.

There was a cool bar in Carmel
where people and dogs got on well.
The dogs were well-groomed
and the music well-crooned,
and they liked her, Carina could tell.

Carina liked to be in Carmel
where the air had a nice ocean smell.
She was welcomed in stores
like all with four paws
and adored the view from the hotel.

Her parents would take her to dine out
if the place had a "Dog Friendly" sign out,
but she stayed under the chair,
with no food she could share.
Why they liked this she never could find out.

As you can imagine, the focus of three elderly beings assisting one another
in independent living is often on the basics: food, water, bathroom habits,
and the occasional complaint about the heat. Occasionally, there is the
existential thought: "Who am I, and why am I here?"

There once was a dog who loved water.
In fact, she drank more than she oughta.
When there was no more
she would scratch at the door,
despite what her parents had taught her.

Carina the dog like to pee
in the closet where no one could see,
but she stayed on the mat.
Dad was thankful for that,
and Mommy would strongly agree.

Carina got up in the night
and walked down the hall for a bite.
But her bowl, it was bare,
with no food anywhere,
so she barked to say "This is not right!".

Carina the dog was impatient
when minnows and treats weren't adjacent.
She'd look up from the floor
with her eyes, she'd implore,
hoping more food would be nascent.

Carina worried 'bout getting her fill
with mommy in bed feeling ill.
Instead of couscous and meat
with a nice minnow treat,
she might just have to eat Daddy's swill.

Carina loved eating her dog food,
and knew that it had to be well-chewed.
There was couscous and meat,
and a small minnow treat.
It always puts her in a good mood.

Carina loved to sleep on the floor.
It was cold, and it cooled every pore.
She was very content,
had no reason to vent,
until somebody came to the door.

Carina did not like the heat.
It bothered her lungs and her feet,
so she lay on some ice,
which felt very nice,
and thought, "Who says the heat can't be beat?!"

Carina climbed into the sink
but knew what was wrong in a wink.
Her smile turned to frown
when she couldn't get down.
Next time, from her bowl she will drink.

Carina's mum did not like bright light.
It bothered her eyes in the night,
so she turned down the dimmer
till there was only a glimmer
and then closed her eyes very tight.

There were few things that mommy could eat,
or she'd hurt from her head to her feet.
No tomatoes or peas,
red meat or cow cheese.
It was hard to get mommy a treat.

Carina did not want to get ill,
so she asked mom to give her a pill.
But mom said 'not yet"
till we check with the vet
to see if there was a refill.

Carina's mom stayed in her bed,
with a pillow and ice on her head.
She said something 'bout Covid,
and mentioned Paxlovid,
and left any more details unsaid.

Carina's mom felt very ill,
with aches, pains, high fever and chill.
Carina tried to get med
to take to Mom's bed,
but was unable to pick up the pill.

The dog hated when mommy was gone.
It made her feel sad and forlorn.
She would sit by the door
until mommy, she saw,
then jumped up, and zoomed 'round the lawn.

Carina loved taking a nap
on the bed or on somebody's lap,
or she'd lie on the floor,
and sometimes would snore.
If mom stirred, she'd wake up ASAP.

Carina would climb on dad's chest
where she'd stretch herself out for a rest.
She did it each morning
without any warning,
thinking this bed was the best.

The dog's daddy liked feeding the birds.
He spoke to them using their words.
He'd say "tweet tweet" and "coo,"
and sometimes, "who! hoo!"
They loved it and came by in herds.

LEAN ON THE DOORBELL
UNTIL A SMALL DOG BARKS

Dear FedEx,

Hi! Hope you are having a good enough day to take a moment to think about this:

> PLEASE DON'T MAKE US DRIVE TO FEDEX AT
> ONTARIO AIRPORT TONIGHT AT 6 P.M.!

Laurence Hoffmann regularly gets shipments from LAFELTRINELLI INTERNET BOOKSHOP and most of the time we are home but someone in a FedEx uniform gives up before we can get to the door to accept the package and then we have to drive to the FedEx facility near Ontario Airport, on the freeway at night and we are too old for that.

If you agree to help us out, you have two options:
Here is all of the paperwork proving it's us including our signatures with today's date accepting the package and waiving all liability for you, FedEx, and La Feltrinelli Internet Bookshop

or

Lean on the doorbell until you hear a small dog bark,
and then our phones will be giving us a signal that the doorbell
is ringing,

and then we will be trying to find our phones,

while trying to calm the dog, let alone leash the little energetic bugger,

and then we will be gingerly easing out of our chairs

so as not to fall over or dislocate anything,

and then we will be reaching for anything else we might need,

glasses, Star War lightsaber walking stick, panic button,

before we start walking towards the hallway

and it is a long indoor hallway,

and yes, we are very grateful we to still be in our nice home.

Thanks for thinking about that,

and then we have to open the door to the outside,

and then we have to unlock the screen door,

and then we have to walk some more,

as there is an outdoor walkway,

and then we have to open the door with two hands,

and remember, we still have our 5 lb. watchdog on leash,

and then and only then,

if you are still there,

will we smile and say, "Hi,"

and gratefully and gracefully sign for and accept the package in person,

and personally thank you,

that is, if you are still there,

and we know you have a lot to do,

quotas to meet, schedules to keep.

So, for everyone's sake, we hope you choose option one,

and we will gratefully and gracefully accept the package in absentia.

Continue on a great day,

Sincerely yours,

Janice and Larry (Laurence) Hoffmann

MASSIMO'S DOGGEREL

Shortly after we lost Carina, we were already talking about our next dog. Why? Because we simply did not want to live without a dog. Massimo was born on January 6, 2023, and he came to live with us when he was nine weeks old. Different from any of our other dogs, he is a strange mixture of neediness and fierce independence, but then, aren't we all?

Massimo sure knows his mind.
Truly he's one of a kind.
He east when he chooses,
picks in which bed he snoozes.
A better dog's quite hard to find.

Massimo came on the scene,
and in dog years, he now is a teen.
He eats all his food
but doesn't grow as he should.
He remains tiny and lean.

Massimo did not gain weight
despite all the dog food he ate
the turkey was nice,
but he spit out the rice
for a plump dog, we'll just have to wait.

Massimo plays with his food
When we'd rather it be well-chewed
It is served on a plate
But is moved to the slate,
yet, when gone, its absence is rued.

Massimo is very good;
He does everything that he should.
He sits, and he stays;
He runs, and he plays,
but he still doesn't eat enough food.

Massimo came down with fleas.
His skin itched like busy bees,
so we went to the vet
(that's a doc for a pet),
and got powders that put him at ease

Massimo went to the vet
They poked him and pinched him, and yet,
He did not complain
and endured every pain
All in all, he is such a good pet

Massimo loves his routine,
For order he is very keen.
He wants a replay,
like in Groundhog Day
And avoids things that are unforeseen.

The gardeners were out on the lawn,
but Massimo wished they were gone.
They mowed, and they blowed,
and they raked, and they hoed.
He thought that they stayed much too long.

Massimo barked at the door
but wouldn't say what he saw.
(It rhymes if you have a NY accent.)
A cat or a bear? Or maybe a hare?
We wish he would use his words more.

Massimo likes to be mindful.
The practice makes him feel kindful.
He sits, and he knows it;
is calm, and he shows it.
He feels strong, like the tower of Eiffel.

Massimo watches TV.
"Slow Horses" & "Professor T."
He likes a good story
if it isn't too gory,
but colors he never can see.

Massimo went to Palm Springs
to find sunshine and cacti and things.
He lay by the pool
And obeyed the gag rule
And never left mom's apron strings.

Massimo's such a good boy.
His lamb is his favorite toy.
He throws it around.
And then rolls on the ground.
Watching him brings us great joy.

"A box came from Chewy.com!

I hope it's a present from Mom!

It is! A new bed!

It feels good on my head!"

Massimo knows how to turn on the charm.